Strategies

of

Power

*Equipping Believers for
Revival and Reform*

Barry A. Cook

A unique compilation of anointed words of study
for The Believer, The Student, and The Minister.

Unless otherwise indicated, all scripture quotations are from the *New King James Version* of the Bible.

Strategies of Power for Pastoring God's People
ISBN: 1-890820-01-6

Revised & Reprinted 2002
Published & Copyright 2001
Battlecry Press

If you would like further information regarding the author, please write to:

Dr. Barry A. Cook
Ambassador Family Church
4055 Oceanside Blvd. Suite T
Oceanside, CA 92056
afc@ambassadorfamily.com

Contents

In its second reprint, this simple book has proven to be an effective and powerful tool in the hands of God's leaders. This is by no means a comprehensive examination of the topic of pastoring for two important reasons:

First, I wanted the material in this book to be useable now and applicable to various levels of Christian leaders.

The second reason is very simple. Although I have over 15 years of pastoring experience and a doctorate degree in church growth and leadership, I constantly find myself in new and challenging experiences. While, I do not pretend to have all the answers, I do recognize the value of learning from every situation. This book shares some valuable nuggets of truth that I have discovered along the way.

Many other topics are covered in the corresponding books of the Strategies of Power series. Each book contains helpful insights for living in the high call that God has designed for you.

Continued success to you, and success to the Kingdom!

Dr. Barry A. Cook

Purpose of the Church

- **Evangelize the Lost**

- **Revival to the Church**

- **Reformation to our Communities**

*I will build My church and the gates of hell will
not prevail against it.*
Matthew 16:18(b)

"Anything less than an apostolic church will not do. In this hour the Lord is releasing an apostolic spirit into the church by restoring the apostolic ministry to the church."

John Eckhardt

And God appointed these in the church: first apostles...
1 Corinthians 12:28(a)

And He Himself gave some to be apostles...
Ephesians 4:11(a)

TRUE APOSTLES ARE COMING

It is true, as you may have heard, that each phase of the five-fold ministry has been, and is being, restored. Our last great surge of the five-fold ministry was the prophetic. The next one is the apostolic. This is not to imply that there hasn't been a degree of these offices already in operation, but there is an emphasis coming on the function and anointing of the apostolic.

This wave of God's Spirit brings God's (not man's) doctrine from the Protestant reformation all the way through the prophetic move of late, and begins to establish, sort out, and set in its proper administration for preparation of the conclusion of this age.

First the knowledge will begin to be brought forth, then the seeds will begin to grow until accuracy of execution is equal to the motives and the character of the apostle.

Then, praise God, divine order and anointing will be released on the level of our New Testament pattern for this office, and possibly even to a greater degree. This means as the glory increases, so will our responsibility. Consider the story of Ananias and Sapphira, the last will be first and the first will be last (Acts 5).

We were built upon the foundation of the prophet and the apostle.

Before we get started, let me state for the record that different apostles have different levels of authority, be it national, regional, or local, and do not have authority over churches or areas that the Lord has not sent them (2 Cor. 10:13).

True apostles are critical to the formation, growth and mission of the message of Jesus Christ.

I am only going to cover portions of the apostolic functions. I encourage you to study the life of Christ, Paul and others under the light of this brief commentary.

As with all of the five-fold gifts, **the apostle is for the edification of the church**. The word **"edify"** means to build up, **to bring structure.** Remember, **everything works by love**.

1. **The apostle is the "general contractor."**
   - His focus is on the whole, and he exhorts and rebukes with all authority.
   - He brings strength to the weak and gives prophetic instruction, caring about every detail as a general contractor does a building over which he is responsible.
   - Carefully following the blueprint, he strategically lays the foundation according to pattern, laws, and codes, laboring fervently to meet the deadline.

Although it may resemble a particular style, the contractor is not the owner. The carpet contractor wants carpet everywhere, the brick contractor wants brick everywhere, the window contractor wants more windows, but **the apostle sees everything according to divine pattern, balanced and in its proper order.**

2. <u>The apostle is a reformer.</u>

- He has to RE-FORM, restructure, improve by change or form, or remove the false or abuses.

God has ordained a proper form, men have moved away from it or built extra. God only blesses what He ordains. The church was formed in the book of Acts through the apostolic anointing. It has been reformed throughout history through the apostolic anointing (Lev. 26:23,24).

Many in leadership are often only concerned with their position and fear losing it. Reform always disturbs those who are satisfied with the status quo and who are leading by soulish control. This is why we must understand the office of the apostolic anointing so that we can prepare our hearts to receive, repent, and reform, not according to man's opinion, but according to Christ, not being confined by soulish preferences.

3. <u>Apostolic anointing is intensely concerned about building believers in God's Word.</u>

NOTE: Scripture references in this section are so numerous just in the New Testament, that I encourage you to do a study on this particular point. You will find the words very strong and pointed.

I am not speaking of man's interpretations, but the doctrines of the Bible and the truths of Christ. Look at Christ's clear teachings and Paul's specific direction and correction concerning proper doctrine.

The very reason why many are sick, confused, and defeated is because of liberal, lost, insecure doctrine.

Most churches lack real unity because they are not rooted in New Testament doctrine and don't really know what they believe.

Unity is not conformity to man's views or opinions. Unity is conformity to Jesus Christ.

4. **The true apostle is concerned with proper order - Holy Ghost, Word-based order.**
   - Martin Luther answered every rebuke with multiple, clear, scriptural truths that declared order and reform in his God-inspired inspired revelation, "The just shall live by faith."
   - Bible truth is that which is found from Genesis to Revelation.

We also need to be ready to give a solid, scriptural defense in humility, based solely on scriptural foundation, not private interpretation to accomodate our present way of doing things.

Another great word to study in scripture is **"order."** If you are really going to study it, you better buckle your seat belt. There is tremendous judgment for not following God's order, and tremendous blessing for following God's order. **Without proper biblical order, God's Spirit will not rest on individuals or ministries.**

5. **True apostles make disciples, not converts** (Acts 14:22; Acts 8:13,18-24; Luke 18:22-29).
   - Because of their love for Christ and His people, they don't hesitate to confront. They have the heartbeat of reconciliation.
   - Condemnation is confrontation without restoration, and is usually born from a root of offense. **If offense is not correctly confronted, it plants a seed and grows into a root of bitterness that hides behind justification, defense, and judgmental attitudes.**

Avoiding Godly confrontation leads to a breeding ground for demons and soulish manifestations that cause strife, division and withdrawal.

Love confronts with proper motives. It is here that apostles, as well as prophets, must keep proper order in their own hearts and check their own motives.

Correction without instruction is ignorance. Instruction without correction breeds rebellion. Authority is never a title or a position, it is a gift from God. There is a big difference between being man-appointed and God-appointed! Whatever we are in Christ, it is by the grace given unto us (Rom. 12:3).

6. **Apostles are spiritual pioneers: pathfinders, trailblazers, and architects.**
- A true apostle does not just speak about being an apostle, he lives it.
- He gets his hands dirty, gets involved, leads the way, and sets the pace often in uncharted water, and often when no one else quite understands what he is trying to say. This is why he must operate from a proper doctrinal, scriptural base; **not trends, opinions or emotions.**

7. **Apostles are concerned with design, structure and form** (I Cor. 3:1-10).
- First, they lay a foundation of proper doctrine and order.
- Then people have to be trained and taught.
- An apostle never suggests or hopes one might just catch on.

Churches have to be organized and governed, not controlled by soulish leaders who are on a power trip. **The leaders should be** those who love God's people and have caught a glimpse of Christ, hear His voice, and who are obedient to the Father's business.

Martin Luther had to correct and even disassociate himself from those who would have taken reformation in the wrong direction (not to imply Luther was correct in all his theology, but the principle was clear).

To pioneer means to open or prepare for others to follow.

- **The apostle steers and pilots the ship, moving forward, setting the pace. He is not passive with false humility, he is not held up by others, nor presumptuous and ambitious.**
- A true apostle moves on God's time clock and not man's.
- An apostle moves rapidly with what he knows. If he is wrong, he corrects it, repents and keeps going.
- He never lets people who don't see the vision tell him that he should calm down, slow down, or change direction. If they do, he corrects them with love and accuracy, or disassociates from them.

NOTE: (Remember, these examples are taken solely from character profiles of New Testament apostles and not from my personal viewpoint.)

8. <u>**Lastly, apostles plant.**</u>
   - They are driven to conquer the fight of breaking through the resistance of a new territory, and they carry the anointing to do it.
   - It is their destiny and they will bear fruit that remains.
   - True apostles raise and develop people to plant new churches.

The Greek word **"phuteuo"** (I Cor. 3:6) means to set in order in the earth, to implant, to instill doctrine.

"Plant" in the Greek implies organizing, developing, nurturing, and strategically planting. It means to actually take responsibility for placing or replacing gifts within the body, the region and the nation. **This is proper order for the apostle.**

Throughout history God has sent the stirring, or the feelings of a movement before the actual position and operation came forth in the earth. **Just because you are sensing an urgency and the need for this office, doesn't mean that you are appointed to this office.**

Don't mistake the "title for the function, or the function for the unction." Ministers should prepare themselves and their people to receive from these true apostles when they come on the scene and begin to enter our churches. Just like anything in its infancy, there will be mistakes, **but get ready...TRUE APOSTLES ARE COMING!**

"The Church was not born powerless, weak, impotent, or anemic - it was born in a demonstration of power, totally dependent upon the Holy Spirit."

Norman Roberts

See, I have this day set you over the nations and over the kingdoms, to root out and to pull down, to destroy and to throw down, to build and to plant.
Jeremiah 1:10

10 CHARACTERISTICS OF A PROPHETIC CHURCH

The devil hates churches and people who flow in the Holy Spirit, because these people are not controlled, they're not held back, and they defeat the devil at every turn. They destroy the works of the enemy and they manifest Jesus. *"For the testimony of Jesus is the spirit of prophecy"* (Rev. 19:10).

I Kings 18:1 (Elijah declared that God would send rain.)
1. **Prophetic Positioning** – A declaration or a pronouncement of something that is to come. Some churches or people spend all their time in a dream world. **Dreaming is not prophecy.** The declaration is only part of the process. <u>You have to work hard and set your vision towards the promised outcome with proper order, discipline, strategies from heaven, faith and strong prayer!</u> **Nothing is free.** The declaration is the only sovereign part, the manifestation may take some time of plowing.

I Kings 18:4, 17-19 (Elijah rose up with a challenge against the false prophets.)
2. **Challenging Spirit** - When a church begins to move prophetically and pray prophetically, you will notice that they always seem to be challenging things. This is the kind of people that God wants us

to be. He told us to go into all the world, He didn't say sit. He didn't say wait until somebody asked you, He said go after them. That's called a challenge! It's a prophetic challenge when a church begins to say, "No, we challenge the principalities and powers that rule over our region." **A prophetic challenge goes out towards two things: 1) the false or counterfeit; and, 2) people deceived by the false.** <u>A challenging spirit cannot be tainted by arrogance, meanness, or haughtiness.</u> **It must be tempered by kindness, love, strength, and compassion, but full of the fire of God.**

I Kings 18:22; 19:22 (I alone am left.)

3. **Prophetic Problems** - There seem to be certain problems that occur among some prophetic churches, and that is the attitude that "we're the only ones, we've got it all together; we're the only ones with the authority; we're the only ones fighting the devil; we're the only ones with the anointing." **You may be, but if that becomes your attitude, then it's wrong.** As we see in the story of Elijah, God doesn't like that, and if there isn't repentance then God will give that mantel to another who doesn't have an attitude. **Nowhere in the Bible did God give prophets a right to have an attitude or to be isolated. Nowhere in the Bible does God give someone the right to be arrogant.** The Bible says the fruit of the Spirit is love, joy, peace, patience, kindness, goodness, faithfulness and self-control. **<u>Every word that is given, every attitude that is presented, has to be tempered by the fruit of the Spirit, or else the prophet is out of order.</u>**

I Kings 18:26-29 (Elijah mocked the false prophets.)

4. **Prophetic Tauntings** - People and churches that begin to move under the prophetic anointing **will taunt the atmosphere with their songs, words, preaching and prayers.** Some people get all freaked out about this when they go into prophetic churches... "Why are they singing that song? Why are they singing against the

devil? Why don't they just sing about love and mercy?" Because that is part of a prophetic anointing that has strength and authority. Its gun is aimed on purpose to destroy the works of the devil. **Jesus is glorified by the spirit of prophecy being the testimony of Christ.**

I Kings 18:30-37 (Elijah rebuilds the altar.)

5. **Prophetic Building** - There are two things that prophetic building does. **First, it builds an altar or a relationship with God; and, second, that altar represents the preparation for the manifestation of the Spirit of God.** Many times preparing yourself enables you to experience the manifestations and blessings of God being poured out on your life. Elijah said to dig a ditch all around the altar and pour water in it. That was so that no man or flesh could perform the miracle or make a way for it to happen. The Spirit of God had to do it or nobody was going to.

I Kings 18:38,39 (Then the fire of the Lord fell....and the people said "the Lord He is God".)

6. **Prophetic Proof** - Elijah had the authority and the proof to back up what he proclaimed. Most people just talk alot, but when it comes down to it, there is no fire coming down, no proof, or fruit. **If you talk the talk, then walk the walk!**

I Kings 18:40 (Elijah gave the order to seize the false prophets and he executed them.)

7. **Prophetic Judgment** - There has been a lot of false prophetic words that have gone on throughout time; however, **there are examples all through the Old and New Testament of the right kind of prophetic and apostolic judgment.** Judgment is for the purpose of putting a stop to something, seizing it, changing it, etc. **When the authority of the word of the Lord comes, it always brings change unto righteousness, then the promise comes.** As people begin to allow the prophetic and apostolic

anointings to operate in their churches, we will see levels of prophetic judgment restored. This is one of the characteristics of a prophetic church. **A prophetic judgment can be exercised towards various things, i.e. principalities, demonic influences, unrighteous governments, crime, sin, hypocrisy, false religion, etc.** Jezebel and the false prophets massacred the prophets of the Lord, thus, a prophetic judgment came forth. Prophetic judgments don't come because of personal offenses. It's not a game, it's serious and must be initiated by the Spirit of God.

I Kings 18:42-46 (Elijah bowed down and put his face between his knees and prayed.)

8. **Prophetic Praying** - This kind of prayer births things into being. It births an anointing, it births a call, it births miracles, it births the promises of God into existence. **It is a kind of prayer that wages war on behalf of the prophecy that comes forth.** Prophetic praying needs to come back to churches and individuals in their homes. **It should be a normal part of our lives.** Prophetic churches need to be churches of prophetic intercession. Prophetic people need to be people of prophetic birthings and intercessions. The devil has skillfully removed this type of praying out of the church. That is how everybody got into all the "user friendly" garbage. That's why the church now tries to please people instead of God.

I Kings 19:1-4 (Elijah fled for his life out of fear because of the threats of Jezebel.)

9. **Prophetic Backlash** - **You can't stop fighting just because you win a victory.** When you throw a punch, expect some retaliation in the spirit realm. **As long as we are on the earth, we will have to fight.** The day that you don't fight, you are going to want to quit and be full of self-pity. Prophetic backlash is a reminder that we are in a war, not a game. The devil isn't going to

sit idly by and allow no resistance against the things of God. **We must take our authority in Jesus Christ and enforce the ways of God in the earth.** You can't live off of the victory or the defeat, you have to live off of your relationship with God.

I Kings 19:13-16 (Elijah went through cycles of victory and defeat.)
10. **Prophetic victory is won through consistency** - People who are inconsistent will have trouble living in the last days. If you are going to remain a prophetic people, you have to operate in prophetic functions in order to stand your ground and live in victory in the last days. **If you don't remain consistent you will turn into an emotional wreck. You will go from victory to defeat all the time.** When you are in a battle against all the enemies of your life, soul and church, you can't live in mediocrity. **Consistency is your only key to victory.** Elijah hid in a cave and felt sorry for himself when the enemy came back against him after the victory.

These ten prophetic characteristics should be applied to our lives with all accuracy. **Our identity is never to be found in titles, positions, or operations. Our identity is found in Christ alone.** *"For in Him we live and move and have our being"* (Acts 17:28(a)).

"If you take away the New Testament pattern of the church, you have no pattern. Then God must send apostolic reformers to re-establish the pattern."

Barry A. Cook

And God has appointed these in the church: first apostles, second prophets, third teachers, after that miracles, then gifts of healings, helps, administrations, varieties of tongues.
1 Corinthians 12:28

THE FIVE-FOLD MINISTRY IN THIS PRESENT MOVE OF GOD

EPHESIANS 4:11-16

From the 1900's until the present, God has skillfully and purposely been building spiritual structure into the earth by releasing various five-fold offices into the spotlight. The revelation and understanding of how they operate and function has been a slow process. It seems as though God released them to function, but there wasn't much revealed knowledge about how these offices were supposed to operate. So then man, as he often does, developed his own job descriptions for these offices and qualified people according to his limited understanding. As a result, when God used someone outside of their "man-made job descriptions" people rose up to fight and discourage God's divine operations. Instead of people going to God and praying for God's revelation and allowing the Holy Spirit to confirm His present will through the Word, they shut God's workings down. One of the greatest mass-examples of this was the 1950's era of the healing evangelists. Men and women evangelists drew huge crowds and people were saved, healed, and delivered by the hundreds. The greater the move of God was fought, the stronger it became.

The church world was baffled by the move of God at that time for three reasons:
1. Most churches were spiritually dead.
2. Many churches were small and sometimes impoverished.
3. The church had no "control" over the evangelists.

We see this same pattern in the move of God that is happening today. Half of the people are fighting against it, and many others have a limited understanding about it or only accept it in part.

There are four typical responses toward the present move of God :
1. A church begins to experience this present move, and they become self-seeking and prideful over it.
2. People try to control and dictate its operation to the degree that they are comfortable, and therefore, it is quickly choked out.
3. It is allowed to operate, but people's hearts are not connected with God's purpose, so it becomes like a carnival or side show.
4. It is deemed as holy, a divine blessing of God's grace sent to confirm His covenant with man. It also renews a love for God's kingdom and a commitment to self-denial, and increases our expectancy for the soon return of our Savior Jesus Christ.

Also, each wave of refreshing contains within it revelation and understanding pertaining to the position of the church in God's overall timetable, as well as information and revelation concerning the changes that the seasonal emphasis brings.

Matthew 13:52 speaks of taking **treasures** from the old and the new. **The emphasis of each refreshing, as well as the basic fundamentals of Christianity, must be active, alive, and in operation in our personal lives and churches.**

All the **treasures** of the past moves of God combined with all the **treasures** of the new are to continue to be applied. **Let me just remind you of these treasures of the past and present:**

- Evangelism
- Diversities of Tongues
- Gifts of the Spirit/Helps
- Administrations
- Faith & Prosperity
- Praise and Worship
- Intercession and all prayer in the spirit
- Deliverance
- Warfare
- Recognition, understanding, and acceptance of the five-fold office gifts.

These are some of the things that have come from various moves of God that we should not let go of, but rather allow to be added as God continues to move in a new and fresh way.

One of the governmental operations that God is focusing on is the recognition, understanding, and acceptance of the Ephesians 4 office gifts. **God Himself is restoring honor, integrity, and a fresh anointing upon the ones entrusted with the awesome responsibility of equipping the saints for the work of the ministry.** God Himself is leading, nurturing, training and releasing a glorious church, a bride without spot and blemish.

Let me tell you several of the **reasons why we often are not able to receive the fullness of God's leadership into our lives and churches**.

1. There is a lack of understanding and revelation of the offices.
2. We are too preference minded. We might not personally like a certain style of leadership.

3. We are insecure with the diversities of ministries. It might rock our comfort zones.
4. We are led by trends and not by the Spirit. We might not be popular with the going church hype.

I want to close with a general overview of each office, and encourage you to receive the offices that are proven and that walk in love and accuracy. Here is a comparison of each office and its characteristics according to the Spirit and the same characteristics when operated in by the flesh:

APOSTLE

Led by the Spirit
- Sets order spiritually, naturally, internally, and externally with structure and sequence.
- Strong and forceful in delivery.
- Very determined to establish the kingdom and lordship of Christ and to remove the spirit of the world, flesh and the devil.
- Sees and hears clearly and usually has very good discernment when dealing with people; maneuvers by the Spirit and is balanced with common sense.
- Anointed to break open territories in the Spirit - 1) Bold preaching, 2) Signs and wonders, 3) Spiritual warfare.

Led by the flesh:
- Gets legalistic, prideful and very self-seeking.
- Feels untouchable because influence is usually strong.
- Their own principles become higher than God's.
- Get comfortable in current position of authority and pace of progress.
- Begins thinking signs and wonders justify bad doctrine, pride, arrogance and lack of fruit in personal character.

PROPHET

Led by the Spirit:
- Sees good and bad in the spirit realm very easily.
- Sees mostly in future tense, but should know proper timings for the fulfillment of what is seen.
- Senses danger and is sometimes very suspicious in a protective manner.
- Despises hypocrisy.
- Anointed to break open territories in the Spirit - 1) Prophetic proclamations, 2) Signs and wonders, 3) Spiritual warfare.

Led by the flesh:
- Gets spacey and unrelatable to people.
- Is self-righteous, judgmental, short-tempered.
- Can be very much led by feelings, and may mistake "feelings" for the Spirit.
- Develops weird, extreme mannerisms, manipulates and selfishly guides people through their prophetic gifting.

EVANGELIST

Led by the Spirit:
- Primarily concerned about winning the lost and discipling Christians.
- Friendly to all.
- Loves the underdog; has a relatability with most types of personalities.
- Has a deep love and respect for the local church, deeply supports and participates.

Led by the flesh: (Evangelist)
- Gets too entertainment minded.
- Gets easily involved in soulish jesting.
- Begins to compromise in various areas.
- May become isolated and experience a lack of vision for the entire Body.

TEACHER

Led by the Spirit:
- Very concerned with doctrine and proper understanding of scriptural and biblical interpretations.
- A dissector of spiritual truths - lays a clear, simple path to walk upon.
- Varies in personality types.
- Expounds upon truths needed or revealed within the church by the apostolic and prophetic.

Led by the flesh:
- Gives information without anointing - interesting but dead, lacking biblical foundation.
- Relies on mental knowledge instead of revelation.
- Very critical of others who don't think, act, or minister like they do.
- Sometimes fights the flow of the Spirit through the other offices.
- Because of a spirit of revelation working in this office, when in the flesh, they veer from the doctrine of Christ into personal revelations not based upon consistent, biblical principles.

PASTOR

Led by the Spirit:
- Has a desire to love and nourish, talk, fellowship, play and work with believers so he can model true Christ-like behavior.
- Is easy to talk to and always has time for others because his/her focus is making disciples.
- Can be compared to the heart of a father towards children - lots of love and lots of correction.
- Sees the need for other ministry gifts to assist and help in the equipping and perfecting of the saints.

Led by the flesh:
- Uses his influence to manipulate people.
- Uses control of others to get favors.
- Gets hurt easily due to insecurity.
- Loses his role as leadership because of familiarity, and stops dealing with blatant problems within the church.

As God brings us revelation about these offices in the Body of Christ and our understanding is enlightened, we can more effectively pray for the fullness of God's leadership to become active in our churches; and thus, be able to accept them and their functions more readily.

Together with this and the continual workings of the Holy Spirit on the inside of **ALL OF US**, accuracy in the Spirit, maturity in Christ, and long lasting revival will be a result. Then we will bear fruit that will remain! Praise the Lord!

"Correction without instruction is ignorance, Instruction without correction breeds rebellion."

Barry A. Cook

...as you know how we exhorted, and comforted, and charged everyone of you, as a father does his own children,
1 Thessalonians 2:11

But we were gentle among you, just as a nursing mother cherishes her own children.
1 Thessalonians 2:7

THE PARENTING SPIRIT

THE HEART OF THE CHRISTIAN MINISTER

*I do not write these things to shame you, but as my **beloved children** I warn you. For though you might have ten thousand instructors, in Christ, yet you do not have many **fathers**; for in Christ Jesus I have begotten you through the gospel. Therefore, I urge you, **imitate me**. For this reason I sent Timothy to you, who is my **beloved and faithful son** in the Lord, who will remind you of my ways in Christ (I Cor. 4:14-17).*

Train up (prepare for responsibility) a child in the way he should go, and when he is old he will not depart from it (Proverbs 22:6 paraphrased).

One of the laws of Genesis is that **everything produces after its own kind.** This is typically true in families, churches and businesses.

We are influenced by those we look up to and learn from. Jesus said a disciple will be like His teacher. The impact of influence is generally based on the quality of teaching.

Jesus is our example of all life and godliness. **He was, and still is, the ideal model of leadership.** His priorities, His focus, the way He instructed, rebuked and encouraged is our ultimate example of a mentor. Jesus exhibits strength, kindness, patience and long-suffering in the Spirit, and reflects the heart of a parent.

One of the many things that God is doing is restoring a heart of true spiritual parenting, both to individuals and corporately to the church.

When someone is truly committed to a cause, they live it, eat it and breath it. It is their lifestyle. It is not mere words of "do as I say and not as I do," which have no mentoring power at all.

When we are committed to a cause, there is clear direction which is motivated by love. You see, this is the heart of a parent that is missing in many homes, churches and ministries. This is one of the missing elements of the church that is being restored.

The church must be the pattern for all aspects of humanity and society. The church has grown slack in producing committed, faithful, Jesus-loving disciples who deny themselves, take up His cross, and follow Him.

As the understanding of the apostolic anointing continues to come into the earth, all those who are tapped into heaven's flow will begin to demonstrate the parenting spirit.

The parenting spirit has a servant's heart. To be a parent in the natural or in the spiritual, is to serve the weaker, younger, and the underdeveloped. In one way, we are all parents, and in another way, we are all children.

Our biblical examples of spiritual fatherhood took a <u>natural</u> responsibility for those under their ministry. The church must understand that it is our **response--ability,** to care for those entrusted to us as a parent would their natural child. <u>We must not lord over them, or use our spiritual position as a tool for feeding our own insecurities,</u> for these are the symptoms of a dysfunctional family. **In the kingdom of God, we must be as little children, innocent, simple, and having the desire to be in the middle of the action.** We also must be continually renewed in the responsibility of spiritual parenting.

Those with parenting spirits give birth, pray for souls, and their hearts are always concerned about the growth and formation of their child (Gal. 4:19). They daily, and without ceasing, pray from a heart of true love and concern, and with tears they long to see and to be with their children (2 Tim. 1:2-5). <u>They also instruct in all areas of life by example with continued support and encouragement.</u>

<u>Here are just a few biblical examples of a parenting spirit:</u>

1. **<u>Daily care -</u>** This is not just a nice thought, it is hard work. How many parents have to make themselves care for their children? Remember that commercial that said, "It's 10:00, do you know where your children are?" Remember God's loaded question of rebuke in Genesis that he asked, *"Cain, where is your brother?"* Cain replied, *"Am I my brother's keeper?"* Jesus said in the gospels, *"He who does not gather with me, scatters."* Proverbs 29:15(b) says, *"A child left to himself brings shame."* **Someone who has the heart of Christ burning within them has a parenting spirit that deeply cares, not just in word, but in action.** Just like a parent cares naturally for their child, it comes natural for a spiritual parent to care for their children.

2.   Helping with weakness -

You who are strong (in your convictions and robust faith) ought to bear with the failings and the frailties of the tender scruples of the weak; (we ought to help carry the doubts, and shortcomings of others and not just to please ourselves) (Romans 15:1, Amp).

Helping, not avoiding, not excluding or isolating. A parent does just the opposite. When a child is weak in certain areas of their life, they work with the child to support and encourage them. Parents do not deny the problem, but help them to develop, even when tough love must be administered.

3.   Helping with strengths - A parent recognizes a child's strengths and, by proper training, sees that they are tempered and developed, spends time with them and gives instruction helping them to mature in their strengths. A parent is also patient with the development of the strength, seeing to it that the strengths are not carried in pride and self-reliance. On the other hand, a child must not be ignored or pushed aside because of failures (Acts 18:24-28).

4.   Providing protection - A parent carries in their heart a desire to see the best for their child. Even when parents send their kids off to school, summer camp, or even military service, they still feel a **response-ability** to help in any way that they can. As the Apostle Paul says, *"Greatly desiring to see you being mindful of your tears, I remember you in my prayers without ceasing"* (I Tim. 1:3,4). This is like keeping a distant, yet watchful eye on your children, being ready at any moment to rescue or provide protection from danger.

5. **Encouraging independence -** This is so we as parents produce children who are a valuable part of society. This is like the parent who makes the child take the candy bar back inside the store and apologize for stealing. Or, taking off the training wheels and pushing the bike, knowing that the child will probably fall, but ready to love and send them back out again. *"...every part does its share, causing growth of the body for the edifying of itself in love"* (Eph. 4:16).

6. **Patience and longsuffering -** A parent must be longsuffering and patient even in the smallest details of development. You can't stop changing diapers, even though you might have been tired of it after only three months. Some things we have to continually remind children of and even show them again and again the proper procedure, with only half of their attention, knowing we will probably have to demonstrate the task again in the future. We do not disown, ignore, or leave them to learn a lesson in their ignorance. I Thess. 5:14 says, *"Now we encourage you brethren, warn those who are unruly (insubordinate or idle), comfort the fainthearted, uphold the weak, be patient with all."*

7. **Love at all times -**

Friends love at all times, and a brother is born in adversity (Prov. 17:17).

"At all times" is very difficult, however, if we truly love our brother, we will tell him the truth. The parenting spirit loves at all times. This does not mean to ignore sin and live in some false, fluffy world of denial. You warn because you love (Eph. 4:15(b))! You encourage because you love. You keep reaching out even when you are rejected (Matt. 5:44). You discipline because you love. You also talk with and are interested in your children, even when you are busy. Why? Because this is the heart of Jesus. This is the heart of a parent.

You see, the parent's job is to build, establish, guide and govern a truth, a home, and a lifestyle. The spirit of a parent says, "minister like this, teach these things, watch out for this." **All the while, it encourages individual identity.**

As a child, no matter how many ballgames I played, my dad always gave me last minute instructions whether I thought I needed it or not. Mom, likewise, was always concerned about how I felt, if I was comfortable, and gave the famous Mom statement, "Be careful, honey."

In reading I and II Timothy and Titus, Paul was giving **specific** instruction, rebuke, correction, and encouragement.

Timothy and Titus were not novices. They had proven ministries, or else they would not have been qualified to be elders or apostles. Jesus and the Apostle Paul were just two that demonstrated the heart of a parent for their spiritual children.

A parenting spirit is also concerned with a move of God, because just as innocence in children is lost, so also a move of God can easily be strangled, polluted and weakened by fleshly and soulish activity labeled "spirit."

- Real parents love their spouse.
- Real parents love their children.
- Real parents love to minister spiritual matters to their family **without dictating their authority. So also the Ephesians 4:11 office gifts must lead the body of Christ.**

Here is how the five-fold ministry operates with the true spirit of a parent:

- The **pastor** tends to coddle and pamper.
- The **evangelist** desires more kids.
- The **teacher** is focused on life's instructions and warnings.
- The **prophet** is quick to bring discipline and present urgencies from the Spirit of God.
- The **apostle** desires internal and external structure and harmony and equality among the family, community and the nation.

"I desire that my first language be tongues and my second language be English."

Roberts Liardon

I thank my God that I speak with tongues more than you all.
1 Corinthians 14:18

WHY ALL BELIEVERS SHOULD SPEAK IN OTHER TONGUES

When Jesus ascended to heaven in His glorified state and sat at the right hand of the Father, it was a sign of His earthly mission being completed. The disciples were instructed to wait until this event had taken place and the Helper was to come after that. It was then that He gave gifts unto man. **All those who call upon the Lord Jesus Christ for the remission of sins are qualified to received the gift of the Holy Ghost** (Acts 1:4-9).

Although scripture speaks clearly about "diversities" of tongues in 1 Corinthians 12, I endeavour in these next few pages to speak of tongues given by the Holy Spirit on the part of a believer as an act of the will (1 Cor.14), praying in other tongues unto God. I am speaking of a **language given by the Holy Spirit as evidence of Christ's heavenly return and the reality of His indwelling presence and power.**

1. **It is the initial sign that are we filled with the Spirit of God.** Acts 2:4 - Tongues is the doorway into a deeper walk with Christ. Tongues come with the package of Christianity (it's kind of like a tennis shoe - they all have tongues). It is the opening to a greater relationship with God.

2. **Spiritual Edification** (I Cor. 14: 4). To build up, a pathway to maturity. It's not the only way, but it is one way. To make internal, structural progress. To build a container, set boundaries and secure proper foundations, a means for the believer to grow up in strength and understanding.

3. **Reveals mysteries and hidden things of God** (Prov. 3:32, Ps. 25:14, 1 Tim. 3:9, II Thess. 2:7, II Thess. 3:16, Col. 1:26, Rom. 16:25, 1 Cor. 2:7, 1 Cor. 6:9). When we pray in other tongues, the things of God are being unfolded within our spirit. All the things that are held in the secret council of the Almighty are being birthed and charged into our lives. God speaks His wisdom intravenously into your veins. It bypasses our natural wisdom.

4. **It reminds us of the Spirit's job description** (1 Jn. 14:13,14). Be assured that God is leading and guiding you into all truth, and showing you things to come. One of the things you can be assured of when you pray in the Holy Ghost is that the guidance of the Holy Ghost is being released into your inner man. At the right time, the Spirit will manifest Himself to give you wisdom and knowledge to be able to overcome and guide you through the storms of life.

5. **Praying in tongues will keep our prayers in line with God's will** (Rom. 8:26,27, Eph. 6:18). When we pray in other tongues we are lining ourselves up with the plan, will and purpose of God. His Spirit in our spirit searches His heart for our lives and helps bring God's divine assignments into our lives.

6. **Praying in the Spirit stimulates our faith** (Jude 20). "...building yourself up with your most holy faith." That is the same meaning in the Greek as that of charging up a dead car

battery. Electrifying! Keeping our faith on fire with the revelation of Jesus Christ.

7. **Makes our spirit more sensitive to sin** (John 16:9-15). As we grow in the Holy Spirit it only stands to reason that the reaction caused is more holiness unto God. The Spirit's constant concern is to present a matured, faithful believer on the day of judgment.

8. **Helps you to pray for the unknown** (Rom. 8:26). With intercession and groanings that can not be uttered. He can pray through us for things that our natural mind has no knowledge of. When words have run out, but our heart still aches with a burden, the spirit of intercession and groaning in other tongues stands in the gap and pulls divine intervention into the circumstance.

9. **Gives spiritual refreshing** (Is. 28:11,12). There is rest and refreshing in the presence of God. Praying in tongues is meant to refresh and bring the peace and joy of God into our vessel, which enables us to endure persecution and suffering associated with life.

10. **A way to give thanks and praise to God** (I Cor. 14:15-17). Gives praise directly to God from your spirit by the Spirit. Praise puts your hand on the neck of the enemy and keeps God in His rightful position in your life. It causes the tangible presence of God to clothe your life.

"The fire of God will melt the fear and indecision at our core and forge a 'can do' conviction that will carry us to our designated triumph."

Mario Murillo

I have come to send fire on the earth, and how I wish it were already kindled!
Luke 12:49

THE FIRE OF GOD

It is vital that we keep our spirits active. It takes a conscience effort to keep ourselves in a place of zeal and spiritual progression. We must - (1) put on the Lord Jesus Christ, taking on a lifestyle conducive with the character of God; (2) make a choice by our will and stay on fire for Jesus; (3) keep our spirit-man stirred up; and, (4) stay focused.

Every spiritual blessing is found in Christ. Going to church and reading your Bible are outward actions of an inward change. The world, the flesh, and the devil try to come to pull against your spiritual life in Christ. When we disallow those hindrances, we will walk in a position where the refreshings of the Lord are upon us. When the glorious power and presence of His Spirit are with you, then you're walking in the "In Christ" position.

The Fire or Zeal of God Comes When You:
- Stay humble.
- Keep your flesh on the altar (crucified).
- Allow Him to use you for His kingdom.

What Happens When We Are Disobedient:
- The heavens which are over you shall be bronze, and the earth under you shall be as iron (Deut. 28:15-23).

- Disobedience or carelessness grieves the Holy Spirit (sin and self are two primary things that grieve the Holy Spirit).

When The Heavens Are Shut Up, Three Things Happen:
(Deut. 11:17)
1. No rain (presence of God).
2. No produce (no fruit of His will).
3. You will perish quickly (spiritual death).

How can you go from a glowing fire of joy in God and happiness in Jesus, and all of a sudden begin to deteriorate down into fleshly piles of aggravation and boredom, with all kinds of garbage over you? It's because you got off the altar and took matters into your own hands. **You are not keeping yourself as a living sacrifice to God.** Jesus said, *"Abide in me and I'll abide in you" (John 15:4).* It's a two-way street. *"Submit yourself unto God, resist the devil and he will flee"(James 4:7). "Draw near to God and He will draw near to you" (James 4:8(a)).*

5 Purposes of the Holy Spirit being UPON You:
(Acts 2:2-4, II Samuel 1:21)
1. Fire (power).
2. To see visions.
3. To grow in your relationship with God.
4. To provide the joy and strength of God.
5. To be in a constant abiding state with God.

The Purpose of the Holy Spirit IN You:
1. A witness.
2. Teaches.
3. Reveals.
4. Helps.
5. Assists.
6. Unknown tongues to pray the perfect will of God.

Selfishness does not produce fire. There is <u>no</u> replacement for the fire of God; no replacement for the tangible presence of God.

<u>Without the fire:</u>
1. You become works/duty oriented.
2. Your flesh rises up to take control on a continual basis.
3. Your mind gets confused constantly.
4. You become easy prey for the devil's attacks.

<u>Advantages of the fire of God:</u>
1. The conscience presence of God is with you.
2. You see clearly, because darkness is pushed back where the fire is burning.
3. Works of darkness are exposed and brought to light, in yourself and in others.
4. You receive warmth from His presence against:
   the coldness of religion,
   the coldness of this world,
   the coldness of relationships,
   the coldness of the flesh.
5. Your ministry and function in the Kingdom shines bright and affects more people.
6. You feel alive in Christ and you freely express Him:
   - Fellowship - you love.
   - Offenses - you forgive.
   - Worship - easy and enjoyable.
   - Praise - bursts forth from your being.
   - Testify - you can't help but preach it, your words are endless.

<u>How To Keep The Fire of God From Going Out:</u>
1. Be sensitive to the Holy Spirit.
2. Repent whenever necessary.

3. Recharge whenever it begins to wane, get back in there with God.
4. Discern the difference between religion, pride, soulish zeal, and true spiritual order.

SELF - EXAMINATION:

How Do I Know The Difference Between The Fire of God and Soulish Zeal?

1. You're carnal one minute and spiritually zealous the next minute. Going back and forth is not the fire of God.
2. You lack the love and tenderness of God. You can come on real strong, but you really can't love everybody.
3. You lack clear biblical direction and revelation.
4. You experience heavy mixtures of pride, arrogance, personal preferences and opinions. It mixes with scripture and sound reason. **What do you do if you recognize it? You climb back on the altar.** Admit it, repent of it, and let God come back on you again. He will purify you and increase the fire.
5. Soulish zeal - you can get real loud and obnoxious, and you are irritated easily when expressing your views. There's nothing wrong with preaching the gospel, but every time you start preaching you sound aggravated and mad, and have a million different personal preferences or opinions. Religious pride is a major enemy.
6. You go into "super spiritual mode," to control and manipulate a situation. It's an attitude problem that can be read easily on people's faces.

Story of a Missionary:

A missionary with his wife and children were working in an isolated area of the jungle of Africa. They were warned that each night as the sun would set, they must build a fire and face the opening of their tents toward the fire. They were to be sure that the fire was blazing and did not go out during the night. If the fire went out, the lions would come into the tent and eat them. One day was an especially long, hard day of traveling and evangelizing. At bed time the missionary had a big, blazing fire burning. Normally, in the middle of the night, the missionary would get up and throw fresh wood on the fire, in order to keep a big blaze going. But this night they were very tired, and in the middle of the night the fire began to wane. The lions that were on the perimeter of the camp began to come closer. The missionary family did not know that the fire had gone out. A lion came into the tent, drug the man out of the tent by his head, and ate him in front of his wife and children.

Be sober, be vigilant; because your adversary the devil walks about as a roaring lion, seeking whom he may devour (I Peter 5:8).

When you don't have the fire of God in your life, your adversary the devil walks about as a roaring lion, seeking whom he may devour. When the fire of God has gone out in your life, the devil has easy access to go into your tent and chew you up. When you have the fire of God burning, it will keep the flesh, the world and the devil at bay. **We have to make a commitment to be a church and a people on fire, where the glory of God dwells in our midst, where the presence of the Lord is around us and with us.**

"You will not inspire others to follow you, *unless* you are a person of *absolute conviction.*"

Barry A. Cook

...it pleased God through the foolishness of the message preached to save those who believe.
1 Corinthians 1:21(b)

HOW TO DELIVER A SPIRIT FILLED SERMON

Herald and preach the Word! Keep your sense of urgency [stand by, be at hand and ready], whether the opportunity seems to be favorable or unfavorable . [Whether it is convenient or inconvenient, whether it is welcome or unwelcome, you as a preacher of the Word are to show people in what way their lives are wrong.] And convince them, rebuking and correcting, warning and urging and encouraging them, being unflagging and inexhaustible in patience and teaching.

(2 Timothy 4:2, Amp)

I. Elements of a Good Sermon:

A. Prayer - Impact and impartation of message revolves around this very point. If you burn with the zeal of God, men will burn also.

B. Scripture - Scripture is the launching pad for projecting truth. It's living and powerful.

C. Proclamation - Must be bold, strong and filled with the vision and passion of God.

II. The Introduction:

A. Relate - Story, illustration or shared burden.

B. Problem - Don't give it all, unfold and make clear the problem.

C. Prophecy - Begin to allow the Spirit of prophecy to flow with divine hope and truth.

III. The Impact:

A. Proof - Scripture that bears witness of God's views.

B. Power - How does this apply to them?

IV. The Revelation:

A. Reality - Hit them between the eyes with the truth of God to enlighten them.

B. Understandable - Make sure it's clear and in broken down terms. Religious talk doesn't impress, reality does.

C. Spirit Led - Watch their reactions and feel your spirit to know if it's time to close or continue. Use a practical illustration and make it so very clear that anyone can understand.

V. The Invitation:

A. Conviction - When truth hits, wrong is seen and felt.

B. <u>Repent</u> - Have humility and be honest before God (Luke 13- unless you repent, you perish, for God resists the proud).

C. <u>Take Action</u> - If it's real, they will be willing to raise a hand, come forward, pray a prayer, change their life.

"The heartbeat of this (new) generation is to press on past the religious hype and entertainment to a place where God's presence is."

Richard Perinchief

I was glad when they said to me, "Let us go into the house of the Lord."
Psalm 122:1

THE SECULAR CHURCH vs.
THE SPIRITUAL CHURCH

In every revival or move of God there is "a David company" of leaders and followers. This is a group of people that is being prepared to take a throne of leadership in a move of God, a revival of God and a reformation. God is designing people for tomorrow's church, because we are not ready for what tomorrow will bring in our present condition (Acts 13:21-25).

It's easy to settle for the old system or order of doing things. The world is constantly coming into the church and making it a **"secular church."** That means it's molded by secular society - in business principles, success, relationships, etc. **The message of the "secular church" is easier to accept and more palatable for them to swallow.**

In the **"spiritual church"** the eternal word of God is delivered by the Spirit of God into a people, and the people respond with a like spirit of God in agreement with it. God is looking for a people that are after His own heart, not the latest trend or book.

Essentially, there are three types of leaders operating in today's Christian world: **Sauls, Jonathans, and Davids.**

1. **Saul = The Secular Church. The old system and old order. Not interested in the new and does everything they can to come against revival and reform.**

- Saul always looked for ways to compromise when he didn't understand something or when he became impatient.
- He always wanted personal confirmation that what he was doing was right, even when the word of the Lord came to him telling him otherwise.
- Saul loved pleasure more than God.
- Saul always wanted to please people instead of being obedient to God.
- Saul lived a life of mixture and inconsistency. Wanted to look good on the outside and was full of sin and devils on the inside.
- Fearful in battle. Where was he when Goliath came around? There were a lot of troops waiting for somebody else to save them.
- Came in and out of the anointing as others affected him (I Sam. 10:10). He didn't live anointed.

2. **Jonathan = An advocate of the old (Saul/secular church), but a protector of the new (David/ spiritual church). Likes to visit with the new, but holds on to and always goes back to the old.**

- For Jonathan to take a stand would mean a loss of position and present status with Saul.
- He sold out so he could be promoted by Saul.
- He was caught between his allegiance to the old existing order, and his association with the new.
- Wanted to be a part of the new, but couldn't let go of the old, which resulted in compromise.
- Looked like so-called revival leaders of today who talk the talk but don't walk the walk, but who usually have great potential.

- Good people, but feel they have a reputation to uphold which causes compromise.
- Can be trusted not to say anything too radical that might rock the boat.
- Can't imagine that God would bring judgment on the system they have a relationship with.
- They love the new, but just can't let go of the old.
- They live with Saul (the old, religious, dead church), but sneak out to be with David (the revived, alive church).
- Double-mindedness keeps them on the side of the Saul. The problem with siding with Saul, is that when judgment came, it came on the "house of Saul." <u>Jonathan died with Saul</u>.

3. **David = The Spiritual Church. A living organism of revival and reform where the Spirit of God flows freely and progression is evident.**

- The process and establishment of the new order.
- David endured with great patience and forbearance until he was made king of Judah.
- David constantly loved and respected Saul and even cried when he died, even though Saul constantly came against him.
- Learned to be faithful over those given under his charge. Shepherd of a small flock of sheep.
- David never allowed Saul's treatment of him to make him bitter or rebellious, or else he would have disqualified himself to lead God's people.
- After being anointed to lead Judah, David then had no hesitation to wage war on the house of Saul (retaliation was not going to be rebellion, it was time to take it by force by the authority of God).
- Patiently waited, with a right heart, for God's perfect timing of promotion for him.
- Learned how to defend his sheep fearlessly from bears and lions.

LESSONS TO LEARN:

1. God is preparing a new order for the end-time church.

2. Learn now what is required for the future. Don't resist.

3. Rid yourself of all rebellion and compromise through patience and loyalty to God.

4. Prepare for battle.

5. Compare your current structure, methods and attitudes with scripture, and field test what you are getting from God.

6. Become teachable in faith and obedience.

7. If you are truly committed to Christ, you won't be a Saul who compromised with the dead, old order; nor, a Jonathan who played both sides of the fence.

8. Be a David who is being trained and training others to function in the new, who has a heart after God and a desire to be obedient above all things.

9. Keep rebellion out, wait patiently as anointings are being released into the earth so that you can rise to take your position at the right time.

10. Be filled and consumed with the Holy Ghost and be yielded and obedient to the Spirit of God.

I heard a pastor once say that if he had to do it all over again, he would be free in the Spirit, but he has spent too much time building his ministry around himself. Thus, he fears he might lose too many people if he tried to change things now. Instead, he has settled for the Saul order, which means he will also settle for the judgment that comes with it.

> *Now there was a long war between the house of Saul and the house of David. But David grew stronger and stronger, and the house of Saul grew weaker and weaker (2 Sam. 3:1).*

"There are many Christians who are Christian in theory only, and they are worldlings in practice."

John Alexander Dowie

Enter by the narrow gate; for wide is the gate and broad is the way that leads to destruction and there are many who go in by it.
Matthew 7:13

KNOWING THE STATE OF
YOUR FLOCK

There are basically three kinds of people in and around the church. Sheep, goats, and wolves (Matt. 25:31-46 & Matt. 7:13-20). **Everyone should prayerfully come to the place where they can be described as sheep.** The following comparison will help you evaluate your progress in the Body of Christ as preparation to be that spotless bride continues. **For it is our love for God that propels us forward and motivates all that we do.** Our relationship with the Lord determines our level of service in His kingdom, and the same principle applies to the church.

Carefully read the 10 characteristics that describe sheep, goats and wolves. This information will enlighten you, minister to you, and stir you to make the appropriate changes in your life.

SHEEP
Spirit-led, Christ-like & humble.
(Matt. 25:31-46)

Purpose: To encourage the sheep to stay humble and repentant, and to assure you of your eternal home.

1. Disciples (teachable).
2. Followers of Christ (servants).
3. Love to be with the Lord (prayer, fellowship, church).
4. Labor with a heart of a servanthood and love.
5. Givers of time, love, mercy , money, care.
6. Tenderhearted, forgiving, relate to all kinds of people.
7. Peaceful, humble, esteem others better than themselves.
8. Naturally reproduce more sheep.
9. Nourish and care for one another, bond together, keep each other warm in cold weather.
10. Heaven bound and Christ minded.

How to deal with sheep: Lead, direct, encourage and support. Bring them close, and care for them.

GOATS
Fleshly, soulish & prideful
(Matt. 25:31-46)

Purpose: To call you to repentance and humility, and to warn you of impending danger and judgment. Goats are middle-of-the-road and can go either way; they can move to be sheep or regress to be wolves.

1. Believers, but moody ones.
2. Followers on their own terms or because of position, person or prestige.
3. Would rather do natural service than spiritual service - more committed to the church than to Christ.
4. Labor from their gift not their heart.
5. Givers with an attitude (depending on feelings, opinions, etc.)
6. Moody; offended easily and often; have weird ways of doing things, which makes them unable to relate to most people. They only run with a select few.
7. Restless and often prideful, see themselves better than others.
8. Only reproduce conditionally and seasonally, and can never reproduce sheep. Draw people to themselves.
9. Easily distracted, does not bond with others, roams, leaves the wounded, and will freeze in cold weather.
10. Unless they change, they will perish.

How to deal with a goat: Gather, constantly prod, exhort, rebuke. Interact and activate, but be ready to correct them of their pride. If permitted, goats will destroy a whole pasture and think they are doing good, yet knowing they are responding contrary to the way that Christ would have things done.

WOLVES
Earthly, sensual & demonic
(2 Pet. 2:10-19)

Purpose: To rebuke, warn, and expose, and to call you to repentance or hell is your destination.

1. May or may not be a believer *("even the demons believe and shudder..." - James 2:19).*
2. Follows for personal gain ONLY.
3. Unlikely to be around church or people unless something is to be gained.
4. Won't labor, only roam about looking for wounded. Hungry to bite.
5. Non-givers, just takers!
6. You never really know where they are. Every relationship is for personal gain only. Their friends are wolves too.
7. Prideful, restless and feel that they are smarter than all others. Knows the "real deal" about life, others and church.
8. Agitate, aggravate, dominate and cause others to stumble with God.
9. Drawn to the wounded, like to eat flesh, hunt the young and the stragglers.
10. Will burn in the lake of fire with the devil and his demons and all those who desire to live ungodly.

How to deal with a wolf: Exhort, rebuke, guard against. Keep a watch for them. Also, capture, corner, expose and warn.

A Word to Pastors

Be diligent to know the state of your flocks, and attend to your herds **(Prov. 27:23).**

"Value excellence in every area of your life."

Excellence can be obtained if you:
Care MORE than others think is Wise,
Risk MORE than others think is Safe,
Dream MORE than others think is Practical,
Expect MORE than others think is Possible,
Work MORE than others think is Necessary.

O Lord, our Lord, How excellent is Your name
in all the earth.
Psalm 8:9

EXCELLENCE IN MINISTRY CHECK LIST

I. WORSHIP SERVICES:

A. Ushers/Greeters -
   1. Professionally and appropriately dressed.
   2. Equipped with breath mints.
   3. Bulletins and visitor packets in hand.
   4. Badges and SMILES on!
   5. Prayed up and anointed to do their job to the max!
      a. Should be able to answer any questions asked about the church, its services, its staff or its pastors.
      b. Should be VERY HAPPY AND SINCERE in their interaction with people.
   6. Ushers should have offering buckets and envelopes ready to go.
   7. Need to be on the look out for any potential problems, BUT DO NOT BE RUDE IN ANY WAY!

B. Platform -
   1. No sloppy cords all over the place.
   2. No litter (i.e. scrap paper, cups, unfolded altar cloths, tapes, etc.).

3. No dead or wilting flowers on the platform. Make them fresh and nice, or do away with them and use artificial greenery arranged nicely.
4. No stray instruments (i.e. tambourines, drum sticks, horns, etc.). Make sure everything has its place.
5. Is there water for the pastor and/or music leader? Put it under the pulpit or on a nice tray sitting on an end table. Don't just put it anywhere to spill or appear to be for public consumption.
6. Keep transparencies and projector in an orderly fashion in a specific place, not just in a pile over in the corner.

C. Auditorium -
   1. Chairs arranged in a uniform way and straightened before service, not after people have begun to arrive.
   2. If you have windows in the sanctuary, keep them clean and clear.
   3. No old bulletins, Bibles, notes, candy wrappers, or personal belongings left week after week in the sanctuary.
   4. General cleanliness is a must, such as vacuuming and dusting.

D. Sound Booth -
   1. The sound booth is not a catch-all for trash/debris loiterers, or teenagers!
   2. Put someone in charge of keeping it organized, neat and tidy. Everything should be in its place, on a shelf, in a box, etc. with labels on everything. Anyone should be able to walk in and identify where something is and what it is.
   3. Batteries and blank tapes should especially be available.

4. WORKERS SHOULD NEVER SLEEP IN THE SOUND BOOTH OR SOCIALIZE DURING SERVICES!

II   NURSERY/CHILDREN/YOUTH:

A. Nursery -
   1. This is a very important area. Mothers must feel at peace about leaving their babies with you. General appearance must be safe, secure, warm, and fun.
   2. There should be enough (HAPPY) workers in this area that no babies are left to themselves to cry while other mothers are dropping off their children.
   3. No unclean smells or appearances should be present!
   4. Bright colors with a soft touch are effective in decor.
   5. Make sure you have appropriate furniture and equipment (crib, changing table, rocking chair, and maybe a walker and/or a swing).
   6. A safety check must be done on all toys and the general play area on a regular basis. NO sharp objects, tiny items that can easily be swallowed, cleaning supplies, food and drinks, etc. should be allowed to go unnoticed!
   7. It is a good idea to have a name and number system for each child and his/her mother.
   8. Ask mothers for any special instructions.
   9. The best way to give security to a mother is for her child to be asleep and at peace or playing happily when she returns.
   10. Do not rely on teenage girls to be your nursery workers. Adults, preferably mothers and grandmothers are a must. It is fine for men to help in the nursery too, but there should always be a woman there. This is not discrimination, but mothers feel more comfortable leaving their children with other women.

11. Diaper bags and contents should be ready to go when mothers return to pick up their babies. Labeling them is helpful.

12. ALWAYS RETURN BABIES WITH A CLEAN/DRY DIAPER, FULL TUMMIES IF A BOTTLE HAS BEEN PROVIDED, AND APPROPRIATE INSTRUCTIONS FULFILLED.

13. Have a system to retrieve mothers from the service if their child is severely unhappy, sick, or uncontrollable. DO NOT take a crying baby to their mother in the service, discretely get the mother to come to you.

14. Clean and disinfect toys after each service (this is easily done in a dishwasher). Also, wash all linens from changing tables, beds, bibs, cloth diapers or towels which may have been used over the shoulder with infants, etc.

15. Spray room with Lysol at each cleaning (it's most effective for killing the cold and flu viruses). Don't spray or use chemicals just before children arrive or while they are present! Don't leave old cleaning rags with chemicals on them laying around!

B. Children's Church - Youth Department -

1. Make sure that whoever is in charge of these areas of ministry is both spiritually and naturally capable. This is not a baby-sitting service or just an entertainment center. It is a ministry. Children and teens must be offered salvation, Holy Spirit baptism, healing, deliverance, etc., as well as fun and fellowship!

2. Review all curriculum to be taught. If the teachers are responsible for their own lessons, make sure you (the pastor) know what is being taught.

3. Always look for fruit in these ministries. You should see regular and frequent evidences of the gifts of the Spirit in

this area of ministry. Children and teens should be being saved, filled, healed, delivered, etc.

4. Children's church and teen facilities should look inviting, exciting and safe to them and to their parents.

5. Teachers should be friendly, fun and on fire for Jesus!

6. Keep a healthy rotation going in children's church, long enough for children to establish trust, but short enough so teachers don't get burnt out.

7. Children and youth cause a church to thrive. Don't ever get too comfortable or put this ministry on the back burner. They are our revivalists and reformers of the future and we have an accountability to God for them.

8. The teenagers of the church MUST be discipled - not just entertained!

9. Whoever is in charge of the teen ministry should be mature (not a novice themselves), and able to handle, by the anointing of God, the challenges of today's teens.

10. Always make sure you have the proper insurance, liability/waiver forms for church activities, and complete the appropriate background checks on all workers for this ministry. Most insurance policies require these things, DON'T TAKE THIS PAPERWORK LIGHTLY!

III   MISCELLANEOUS

A. Always type signs, labels, handouts, sign-up sheets, etc. Don't just handwrite or draw information like this. Make it look nice and professional. Your church may not be very big or have very many office machines, but every town has at least a "Kinkos" or something comparable and inexpensive.

B. **NEVER, EVER**, allow your receptionist or office workers to answer the phones rudely or deal with people in the office or over the phone with an attitude! Not only is it unprofessional, but shows a great lack of the fruit of the Spirit. This is not too much to ask for a church office. Just like in the business world, first impressions are lasting ones!

1. Always post current information by the phone or in the office so whoever is answering the phone can give thorough and accurate responses. Never allow responses such as "I don't know, that's not my job or department" to be tolerated as acceptable.

2. Hold monthly or bi-monthly training sessions or workshops for office, music, and other department leaders to carry out the vision and then declare it with the same voice in every area of ministry.

C. Make sure the outside of your building or facilities is kept attractive, clean, and professional looking as well. Keep litter picked up, grass cut, exterior paint fresh, signs lit or painted nicely. There is always a way to make the most out of what you have!

D. ALWAYS keep the bathrooms clean, sanitary, sweet smelling, stocked with supplies, and nicely decorated. The heart of a ministry is often revealed in other places besides the pulpit. No rusty faucets, broken toilets, leaky sinks, etc. You wouldn't like this in any business or restaurant you visited, and it especially shouldn't be a standard in the house of God.

"People of excellence are people of growth."

Rick Godwin

"Excellence is the gradual result of <u>always</u> striving to do better."

Pat Riley

**"You must first
possess your soul,
if you want to
possess your land."**

Troy Marshall

*By your patience possess your souls.
Luke 21:19*

WHAT TO DO WHEN YOU ARE IN DEEP!

Are You In Deep:
Trouble ?   Financial Debt ?
With Wrong Relationships ?
Sin ?   Poverty ?
Depression/Anger ?
Marital Problems ?
Pride ?

7 Ways To Get Out!

I sink deep in mire, Where there is no standing:
I have come into deep waters, Where the flood
overflow me (Psalm 69:2).

1. **STOP!**

   For the wages of sin is death, but the gift of God
   is eternal life in Christ Jesus our Lord (Romans
   6:23).

- Consider your ways.
- Count the costs of your life and the direction it's going. PAY
  DAY WILL COME!

- You <u>will</u> harvest what you sow. Everything costs something!
- Where is my current course taking me and do I want that destination?
- Yesterday's seed is being harvested NOW! Are you prepared for it?
- YOU <u>can</u> STOP it, and you are the only one that can stop it!
- Plow up your field of bad seeds and **replant good ones!**

2. Be Humbly Aggressive.

> *God resists the proud, But gives grace to the humble (James 4:6).*
> *...the kingdom of heaven suffers violence, and the violent take it by force (Matthew 11:12).*

- If you are just humble, you will be defeated, and if you are just aggressive, you will be in pride.
- Humility and aggression must work hand in hand.
- Humility empowers you to build and unashamedly place yourself on the right course in life.
- <u>Attack:</u> When you are in lack - **Attack!**
  When you fail - **Attack!**
  When you are down - **Attack!**
  In order to win you must fight the fight.
- The moment you're not attacking, the devil will lure you away into weakness and pull you off course.
- Attack anger with peace, hate with love, and prayerlessness with prayer.
- God created you to conquer. **Never stop fighting!**

3. Avoid Opportunity.

> *See then that you walk circumspectly, not as fools but as wise, redeeming the time, because the days are evil (Ephesians 5:15,16).*

> *Walk in wisdom toward those who are outside, redeeming the time (Colossians 4:5).*

- Defeat goes to the casual player.
- Don't tell your strategy to those who are fighting against you.
- Be too busy doing the right thing, that you have no time to do the wrong things.

4. Major On Your Strengths And Manage Your Weaknesses.

> *For your obedience has become known to all. Therefore I am glad on your behalf, but I want you to be wise in what is good (Romans 16:19).*

- Change what you can change, and stop worrying about the things you can't change.
- Focus on the things that are clear, not the things that are unclear.
- Deal with things one day at a time, with full effort regardless of others.

5. Leave Room For SHORT Emotional Times.

> *If we confess our sin, He is faithful and just to forgive us our sins and to cleanse us from all unrighteousness (1 John 1:9).*

- "Short" is the key word - **Then Continue!**

- Just because you fall doesn't mean you can't get up!
- It's not important how many times you fall, it's how quickly you get up!
- If God is going to forgive you, don't argue with yourself about it.
- Temporary setbacks do not destroy the whole journey.

6. Look At The Long Term Outcome.

> *Not that I have already attained, or am already perfected; but I press on, that I may lay hold of that for which Christ Jesus has also laid hold of me. Brethren, I do not count myself to have apprehended; but one thing I do, forgetting those things which are behind and reaching forward to those things which are ahead, I press toward the goal for the prize of the upward call of God in Christ Jesus (Phil. 4:12-14).*

> *Therefore, beloved, looking forward to these things, be diligent to be found by Him in peace, without spot or blameless (2 Peter 3:14).*

- Traffic detours and road blocks don't change the prize.
- Daydream and discuss the prize, not the problem.
- Stay moving! When times are tough - fix your eyes on the prize.
- When things are easy - RUN hard and fast, while you have the chance.

7. Purpose Your Thinking: It's Vital!

- The thoughts you entertain will either bring purpose and prosperity, or defeat and lack.
- To change your life you must **make the change** and purpose to do so!
- Actions are directly connected to your thought life.
- Your mind is the battlefield: **rehearse, review and renew,** every morning and every night.
- Rejoice, repent and purpose your thinking.

Finally, brethren, whatever things are true, whatever things are noble, whatever things are just, whatever things are pure, whatever things are lovely, whatever things are of good report, if there is any virtue and if there is anything praiseworthy meditate on these things (Phil. 4:8).

<u>**True:**</u>	Not concealing, agree with the facts, correct, accurate, sincere.
<u>**Noble:**</u>	Revere, adorn, high character.
<u>**Just:**</u>	Innocent, holy, right, see God's will, discuss on a matter, lawful, factual.
<u>**Pure:**</u>	Clean, holy, modest, free from fault or guilt.
<u>**Lovely:**</u>	Friendly, accepting, respect others, strengthen them in Christ.
<u>**Good Report:**</u>	Well spoken, well done, positive, no opportunity for rumor.
<u>**Virtue:**</u>	Excellent, morally pure, God likeness, sexual purity.
<u>**Praise Worthy:**</u>	Encouraging, express praise, worthy of glory.

"At the core of leadership is <u>one single trait</u> - <u>belief in a cause</u>. If you don't believe with all your heart, and all your soul, in what you are <u>fighting for,</u> <u>you will not</u> be a leader."

Barry A. Cook

And since we have the same spirit of faith, according to what is written, "I believe and therefore I spoke," we also believe and therefore speak...
2 Corinthians 4:13

PRINCIPLES FOR ACTIVATING YOUR FAITH FOR LIFE & MINISTRY

Now faith is the substance of things hoped for, the evidence of things not seen.
But without faith it is impossible to please Him, for he who comes to God must believe that He is, and that He is a rewarder of those who diligently seek Him (Hebrews 11:1,6).

1. Do not be moved by what you see or hear, but be moved by what you believe.
2. Faith can be created in others.
3. Faith creates the circumstances of receiving by bold words of faith.
4. Faith can be transferred by the laying on of hands.
5. Faith must be acted upon.
6. Sometimes you must initiate the action for people (i.e. doing something they couldn't do before, sing, dance, laugh, pray loud...etc.).
7. Always use healing testimonies to build faith.
8. When the slightest breath of the Spirit is felt, withdraw to listen and speak to God.

9. If the Spirit isn't moving, move the Spirit. How? BY FAITH!
10. Focus people on the word and power and increase their expectancy.
11. Don't ever wait for something to come upon you. Every action, operation, manifestation is ignited by initiation.
12. Get everyone filled with the Holy Ghost.
13. Cry and weep for the afflicted, care for the elderly and babies.
14. Pray over handkerchiefs and letters with bold faith.
15. Be aggressive against the devil, loud and sudden.
16. Cast out scoffers and strife will cease.
17. Never respond negatively to criticism, increase your faith attack.
18. When before a big crowd, have people lay hands on themselves and believe.
19. Approach everything and everyone with faith in Christ Jesus.
20. Use humor and laugh often, live cheerfully in everything.
21. Don't let personal agonies, struggles or trials slow you down.
22. We don't need more power, we just need to use our faith and compassion for the power to operate.
23. Take God at His word and exercise your faith - step out.
24. Faith is to:
    - subdue kingdoms,
    - work righteousness,
    - obtain promises,
    - stop the mouth of lions,
    - quench the violence of fire,
    - escape the edge of the sword,
    - be made strong out of weakness,
    - become skilled and aggressive in battle,
    - cause God's enemies (flesh, sin, world, devil) to leave running.
25. Stir up the gift of God within you.
26. Faith must be unflinching and sometimes ruthless.
27. Teach the word with an unusual anointing.
28. Keep a keen sense of compassion.

29. Live as a soul-winner.
30. Never leave home without a New Testament.
31. Be a hard worker in everything.
32. Allow your emotions to fervently be expressed during ministry.
33. Fast and pray when seemingly impossible internal or external problems arise.
34. The more fervently God is expressed, the more of a supply it creates in others.
35. Frequently, methods will be criticized and misunderstood - NEVER BE MOVED!

"In his usual strategies, the devil influences his own to seek and function with a counterfeit."

Bobbie Jean Merck

Now the Spirit expressly says that in latter times some will depart from the faith, giving heed to deceiving spirit and doctrines of demons.

I Timothy 4:1

SPIRIT OF THE AREA: DIVINATION

A city's stronghold has everything to do with a city's destiny. Satan cannot change a city's destiny, but he can set up the opposite or counterfeit to hinder it (Matt. 12:22-29).

Our cities are meant to be a strong, spiritual center for the release of God's power. It is for this reason the devil tries to raise up counterfeits, such as New Age, spiritualism, and witchcraft in an area. It rules hearts and affects the mindset of the people. This is called divination, and its purpose is to bring a spiritual death to an area. It brings a lot of false alternatives, false control, manipulation and "curses" in the name of the Lord.

Signs of Strongholds in an Area:
- Rarely any strong, free churches.
- False doctrine governing the area.
- Spiritualism in the area.

Attributes of the Spirit of Divination-Python:
- Always battling - mind is always troubled.
- Weariness, fatigue, tiredness, boredom.

- Confusion, frustration, pressure, doubt.
- Spirit of Divination squeezes you, like a python. It is comparable to a large constricting snake that wraps around you and squeezes the life out.

Divination - called in the Bible "a system of fraud." An abomination to God. Fraud is a perversion of the truth to induce another to let go of something of value, or to surrender a legal right (Deut. 18:9-13, 18 and 19).

Attributes of Divination in the Church:
- Adultery in leadership and people.
- Discord, division, divorce, disharmony.
- False guilt, spiritual manipulation.
- Confines people, restricts - suppression of own feelings, behavior and actions.

Divination - two words that come from it: division, divorce. Spirit of discord and division. The purpose of this spirit is to confine people. Confine means "to bring into a narrow compass, clasp tightly, or to hold back by force."

The Spirit of Divination is accompanied by greed, guilt and control. It sends plagues of distraction, feelings of unworthiness and confusion. **Divination tries to soothe your feelings of urgency and quench the fire of the Spirit of God.**

Divination is a curse - an abomination to God. It sets up spiritual strongholds of division and witchcraft. It corrupts and defiles by mixing beliefs, doctrines, and actions of the world into the church.

Divination offers false peace - New Age comes with a gentle spirit through astrology, false prophecy, mediums, soothsayers, sorcery and spiritualists.

Satan divided heaven and divorced God's covenant. Divination tries to divide you from God's blessing and divorce you from God's covenant (Deut. 7:2-10).

Exposure: Once you expose it, it lashes back with a familiar spirit (past strongholds). There are three typical responses:
1. **Emotional** - tries to manipulate you with false prophecy, false words and slanted praying.
2. **Anger** - lashes out at you with words of failure or defeat and criticism.
3. **Silence** - tries to give you ashamedness or guilt with a false obligation.

Keys to Freedom - Acts 16:
- Radical and sincere praise and worship.
- Strong prayer (praying and singing).
- Make an open declaration of faith in God and the principles of His Word (the prisoners heard them - Acts 16:25).
- Stand for truth, no matter what.
- No compromise in any area.
- Repent for any wrong doing (break free from the past).

You must bind the strong man over the area, city or region. If you're not standing against these things, you are standing with them, and there is still a division in your heart (Matt. 12:22-29).

You must pull down and stand against the stronghold of the area (Ezek. 22:23-31).

Divination must be hit head on, under the anointing and direction of the Holy Spirit.

Select Bibliography

John Eckhardt, *The Apostolic Church* (Chicago, IL, Crusaders Ministries, 1996), Preface.

Norman Roberts, *The Spiritual Church* (Matthew, NC, NRM Publications, 1993), 11.

Mario Murillo, *Fresh Fire* (Danville, CA, Anthony Douglas Publishers , 1991), 80.

Richard Perinchief, *The New Breed Church - In Your Face* (Laguna Hills, CA, Embassy Publishing, 1993), 19.

John Alexander Dowie, *Heroes of Faith* (Tulsa, OK, Harrison House, 1996), 56.

Rick Godwin, *Excellence* (Audio Tape) (San Antonio, TX, Eagles Nest Christian Fellowship), 11/10/96.

Bobbie Jean Merck, *Spoiling Pythons Schemes* (Toccoa, GA, A Great Life, Inc., 1990), 24.

AUDIO SERIES BY DR. BARRY COOK

Sublime Mysteries: Unlocking the Mind of Christ	$20.00
The New Breed Church	15.00
The Power of Prayer	25.00
Transforming the Spirit of Your Home	20.00
True Prophetic Ministry	30.00
Understanding Your Pastor:	
How to Support Your Pastor's Burden	15.00
Vision	15.00
You've Gotta Fight to Stay Right	30.00

BOOKS BY DR. BARRY COOK

Strategies of Power for Pastoring God's People	$5.00
Strategies of Power for the 21st Century Family	5.00
Establishing Your Course Through the Prophetic Anointing	10.00
Prophetic Anointing Study Guide (or Teacher's Guide) each…	10.00
Apprehended by God	2.00

AUDIO SERIES BY PASTOR TERRI COOK

Overcoming the Flesh Factor	$10.00
Called According to His Purpose	10.00
How to Prevail When the Devil's on Your Trail	10.00
Kingdom Keys: Faith, Spirit, & the Word	15.00
Freedom from Strife	15.00
Women of Divine Purpose Conference 2002:	
Breaking Open Your Alabaster Box	25.00

ORDER NOW!

call: (760) 639-4000, fax: (760) 639-4122

Order today at www.ambassadorfamily.com!

AUDIO SERIES BY DR. BARRY COOK

____23 Principles of an Apostolic Mandate	$15.00
____Apostolic Churches & the Antioch Pattern	30.00
____Apostolic Teams: Standard Equipment for NT Churches	20.00
____Ascending the Heights in Prayer	20.00
____Basics of Faith	10.00
____Breaking Soul Ties	15.00
____Bring Back the Glory	15.00
____Changing Wineskins	20.00
____Church Discipline: New Testament Patterns for Restoration	20.00
____Church: It's Not What it Used to Be	40.00
____Coming Out of Egypt: It's Time to Go Forward	45.00
____Crisis: A Force of Increase	20.00
____Dynamics of Spiritual Growth Volume 1 Progressing In Revelation	20.00
____Dynamics of Spiritual Growth Volume 2 From Infancy to Maturity	15.00
____Fourth Quarter Christians	15.00
____Going Through the Fire Without Getting Burned	10.00
____Grace	20.00
____Great Spiritual Leaders of Church History	30.00
____How to Conquer Demonic Powers: Exposing the Spirit of Witchcraft	20.00
____In Defense of the Gospel: Standing for Truth in a World of Hollow Philosophies	20.00
____Living in the Realm of the Spirit	15.00
____Love and the Apostolic Church	20.00
____Mad, Sad or Glad	20.00
____The Origin of the Apostle	20.00
____Pathway to Breakthrough	15.00
____Praise Until Something Happens	20.00
____Prophetic Protocol: Establishing Your Course through the Prophetic Anointing	30.00
____Radical Christianity	20.00
____Rebuilding Apostolic Foundations Volume 1 The Need for Leadership	20.00
____Rebuilding Apostolic Foundations Volume 2 Rediscovering a Life of Power	20.00
____Rebuilding Apostolic Foundations Volume 3 The Price of Good Ministry	20.00
____Rebuilding Apostolic Foundations Volume 4 Restoring Sound Doctrine	30.00
____Renewing Your Mind	25.00
____Revelation Impartation	10.00
____Riding to Conquer: The 4 Horses of Christ's Sanctifying Work	25.00
____Sheep, Goats and Wolves	15.00
____Spirit of Reformation	20.00
____Spirit of the Area: Divination	20.00
____Spiritual Momentum	20.00
____Strategies for Strong Christian Living	30.00

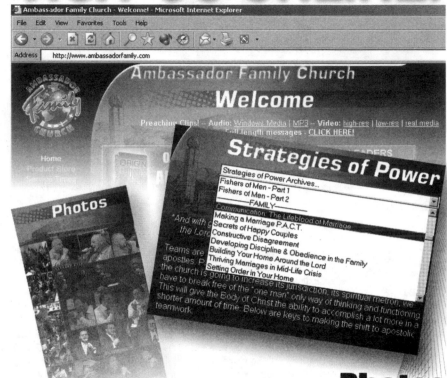